# How to Sparkle at Nursery Rhymes

Jo Laurence

Brilliant
PUBLICATIONS

We hope you and your class enjoy using this book. Other books in the series include:

*English titles*
How to Sparkle at Alphabet Skills                                      978 1 897675 17 5
How to Sparkle at Grammar and Punctuation                             978 1 897675 19 9
How to Sparkle at Phonics                                             978 1 897675 14 4
How to Sparkle at Prediction Skills                                   978 1 897675 15 1
How to Sparkle at Word Level Activities                               978 1 897675 90 8
How to Sparkle at Writing Stories and Poems                           978 1 897675 18 2
How to Sparkle at Reading Comprehension                               978 1 903853 44 3

*Maths titles*
How to Sparkle at Counting to 10                                      978 1 897675 27 4
How to Sparkle at Number Bonds                                        978 1 897675 34 2
How to Sparkle at Addition and Subtraction to 20                      978 1 897675 28 1
How to Sparkle at Beginning Multiplication and Division               978 1 897675 30 4
How to Sparkle at Maths Fun                                           978 1 897675 86 1

*Science titles*
How to Sparkle at Assessing Science                                   978 1 897675 20 5
How to Sparkle at Science Investigations                              978 1 897675 36 6

*Festive title*
How to Sparkle at Christmas Time                                      978 1 897675 62 5

To find out more details on any of our resources, please log onto our website: www.brilliantpublications.co.uk.

Published by Brilliant Publications
Unit 10
Sparrow Hall Farm
Edlesborough
Dunstable
Bedfordshire
LU6 2ES, UK

email: info@brilliantpublications.co.uk

General information enquiries:
Tel:       01525 222292

The name Brilliant Publications and the logo are registered trademarks.

Written by Jo Laurence
Illustrated by Kate Ford
Cover photograph by Martin Chillmaid

© Jo Laurence 1996

Printed ISBN:      978-1-897675-16-8
ebook ISBN:       978-0-85747-091-1

Printed in the UK.
First published 1996. Reprinted 1999, 2005 and 2009.
10 9 8 7 6 5 4

# Contents

# Introduction

This book is one of a set of four devoted to basic strategies which will help early or beginning readers to find their way through the maze of complicated skills which make up the ability to read.

It is widely recognised by reading experts that children who have learned and absorbed the traditional nursery rhymes before they come to school have an advantage when it comes to beginning reading. Extensive research has proved that children who cannot recognise words that rhyme with each other often have difficulties when learning to read. Some children come into school knowing rhymes, some do not. Learning and reciting the rhymes together is an excellent beginning strategy towards the sharing and use of language.

The rhythm of the rhymes helps children to remember the words, which, in turn, helps to develop their auditory memory skills. When they have learned the words and then see them in print they find they can 'read' them. Not only will this give them a greater understanding of how the written word represents the sung or spoken word but it will help to develop their visual memory.

Once the children have grasped the idea of rhyme and rhythm you can play games with them which will give the children even greater skills:

- Give the children rhyming clues (eg 'I am thinking of a word that rhymes with tap and it shows you where you are') and get them to guess what word you are thinking of.

- Make a Rhyme Bag. Fill a bag with simple objects. The children take turns to take one thing out of the bag and they all give words that rhyme with its name.

- Odd-one-out. Give a list of words, all but one of which rhyme (eg 'cat, hat, mat, eye, bat'). Get the children to tell you which one doesn't fit.

- Tap-a-rhythm. Get the children to copy simple rhythms tapped out with a pencil.

- Get them to tap out, or clap, each other's names.

- Tap out the rhythms of specific nursery rhymes for them to identify.

The activities in this book focus particularly upon direction and sequencing because the very nature of nursery rhymes makes them a natural vehicle for the development of these skills. The text has been kept to a minimum so that the children can concentrate upon familiarising themselves with the written form of the words which they already know.

The other three books in this series deal with word recognition and prediction skills, the alphabet and alphabetical order, and phonics.

# How to use this book

The book has been designed so that the children may use its sheets to create their own nursery rhyme books.

There are two pages for each rhyme. One page has the rhyme, clearly typed, followed by activities to develop sequencing and/or direction skills. The second page has a sequencing activity. We envisage the sheets being used as follows:

- Teach the children a rhyme in groups or as a whole class first.

- Give them the first activity page and help them to work through the rhyme and look for all the words they know. At this stage they should be able to 'read' the rhymes.

- The children can then complete the activities. Although the instructions have been kept as simple as possible, you may need to read through the sheet carefully with some children before they start.

- To use the second page of each rhyme they will need scissors, crayons, glue and a blank page to stick the pieces to. Each of the completed second pages should be kept until all the sheets are done, when they can be stapled or tied together for each child to make a book. Page 48 is designed to be used as a cover which may be coloured and illustrated.

Where the words are printed in a pale grey tint, they are to be traced over. Where there is a blank space this is for the children to copy into. Instructions to this effect have been omitted wherever possible so as to leave the pages clear and uncluttered.

The rhymes are all punctuated as they were in original versions. As well as the children learning the rhymes and completing all the activities, you may wish to point out specific punctuation marks and demonstrate how they mean pause, longer pause, etc. Where speech marks are shown, the opportunity may be taken for you to explain their meaning and ask the children who is doing the talking.

The sheets should be used flexibly where they fit in with the other work you have planned. Knowledge of the children's individual needs and of the sheets will help you to provide a balanced and useful programme for each child.

# Humpty dumpty

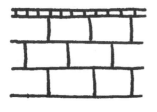

Humpty dumpty sat on a wall.
Humpty dumpty had a great fall.
All the king's horses and all the king's men
Couldn't put Humpty together again.

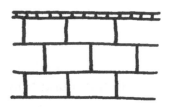

**Continue the pattern.**

_____  _____  _____  _____

**Draw Humpty <u>on</u> the wall.**

**Draw Humpty <u>off</u> the wall.**

**Colour the star
if you can write
a word that
rhymes with
'wall'.**

__umpty __umpty

# Humpty dumpty

**Colour the pictures.**
**Cut them out and stick them in the right order.**

Humpty dumpty had a great fall.

Couldn't put Humpty together again.

Humpty dumpty sat on a wall.

All the king's horses
and all the king's men

# Little Boy Blue

Little Boy Blue, come blow your horn,
The sheep's in the meadow
The cow's in the corn.
Where is the boy that looks after the sheep?
He's under the haystack fast asleep.
Will you wake him?
No, not I!
For if I do, he'll be sure to cry!

---

**Follow the path to find Little Boy Blue.**

**Continue the pattern.**

b d b d

**Colour the star
if you can find
a word in the
rhyme that means
'field'.**

__ittle __oy __lue

# Little Boy Blue

**Colour the pictures.**
**Cut them out and stick them in the right order.**

Will you wake him?
No, not I!
For if I do, he'll be sure to cry!

Little Boy Blue, come blow your horn,
The sheep's in the meadow
The cow's in the corn.

He's under the haystack fast asleep.

Where is the boy that looks after
the sheep?

# Jack and Jill

Jack and Jill went up the hill
To fetch a pail of water;
Jack fell down and broke his crown,
And Jill came tumbling after.

Up Jack got and off he trot
As fast as he could caper;
He went to bed to mend his head
With vinegar and brown paper.

**Trace and draw.**

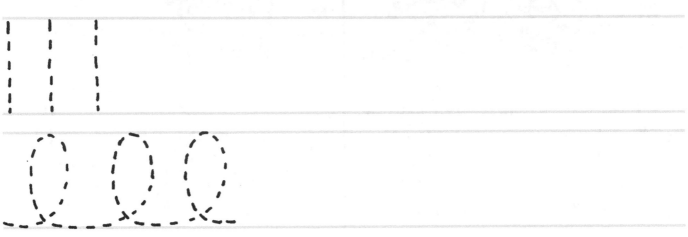

**Continue the pattern.**

up down up down

u

__ack and __ill

**Colour the star if you can find the word 'trot' in the rhyme.**

# Jack and Jill

**Colour the pictures.**
**Cut them out and stick them in the right order.**

Jack fell down and broke his crown,
And Jill came tumbling after.

He went to bed to mend his head
With vinegar and brown paper.

Jack and Jill went up the hill
To fetch a pail of water;

Up Jack got and off he trot
As fast as he could caper;

# Mary had a little lamb

Mary had a little lamb,
Its fleece was white as snow,
And everywhere that Mary went
The lamb was sure to go.

It followed her to school one day,
That was against the rule.
It made the children laugh and play
To see a lamb at school.

**Follow the lamb to school.**

**Continue the pattern.**

## go go

__ary          __amb

**Colour the star if
these words rhyme.
play
day**

# Mary had a little lamb

Colour the pictures.
Cut out the boxes with the words in.
Stick each box of words into the space under the picture it belongs to.

| | |
|---|---|
| It made the children laugh and play<br>To see a lamb at school. | And everywhere that Mary went<br>The lamb was sure to go. |
| Mary had a little lamb,<br>Its fleece was white as snow, | It followed her to school one day,<br>That was against the rule. |

# Old Mother Hubbard

Old Mother Hubbard
Went to the cupboard,
To get her poor dog a bone.
But when she got there,
The cupboard was bare,
And so the poor dog had none.

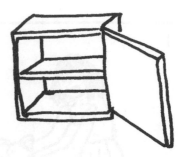

**Continue the pattern.**

d o g d o g

**Find the dog's bone.**

__ld __other __ubbard

**Colour the star if you
can find the word
'cupboard' in the rhyme.**

# Old Mother Hubbard

**Colour the pictures.**
**Cut out the boxes with the words in.**
**Stick each box of words into the space under the picture it belongs to.**

| | |
|---|---|
| And so the poor dog had none. | But when she got there,<br>The cupboard was bare, |
| Old Mother Hubbard<br>Went to the cupboard, | To get her poor dog a bone. |

# Hey, diddle, diddle

Hey, diddle, diddle,
The cat and the fiddle,
The cow jumped over the moon.
The little dog laughed to see such fun,
And the dish ran away with the spoon.

**Can you write the word?**

_____   _____   _____

**Continue the pattern.**

dish fun   dish fun

d

the __at and the __iddle

Colour the star if
these words rhyme:
fun
bun

# Hey, diddle, diddle

**Colour the pictures.**
**Cut them out and stick them in the right order.**

The cow jumped over the moon.

And the dish ran away with the spoon.

The little dog laughed to see such fun,

Hey, diddle, diddle,
The cat and the fiddle,

# Incy wincy spider

Incy wincy spider
Climbed up the spout.
Down came the rain
And washed the spider out.
Out came the sun
And dried up the rain.
Incy wincy spider went climbing up again.

## Draw what happens next.

## Continue the pattern.

sun rain sun rain

s

__ncy __incy __pider

Colour the
star if you can
find a word in
the rhyme that
means
'drain-pipe'.

# Incy wincy spider

**Colour the pictures.**
**Cut out the boxes with the words in.**
**Stick each box of words into the space under the picture it belongs to.**

| | |
|---|---|
| Down came the rain<br>And washed the spider out. | Out came the sun<br>And dried up the rain. |
| Incy wincy spider went climbing<br>up again. | Incy wincy spider<br>Climbed up the spout. |

# Little Miss Muffet

Little Miss Muffet
Sat on a tuffet,
Eating her curds and whey;
Along came a spider
Who sat down beside her,
And frightened Miss Muffet away.

**Continue the pattern.**

_____ _____ _____ _____

**Circle the picture that is the same.**

Colour the star
if you can find
the word 'came'
in the rhyme.

__ittle __iss __uffet

# Little Miss Muffet

**Colour the pictures.**
**Cut them out and stick them in the right order.**

Eating her curds and whey;

And frightened Miss Muffet away.

Along came a spider
Who sat down beside her,

Little Miss Muffet
Sat on a tuffet,

# Sing a song of sixpence

Sing a song of sixpence
A pocket full of rye;
Four and twenty blackbirds
Baked in a pie.
When the pie was open
The birds began to sing;
Wasn't that a dainty dish
To put before a king.

**Trace and draw.**

**Can you write the word?**

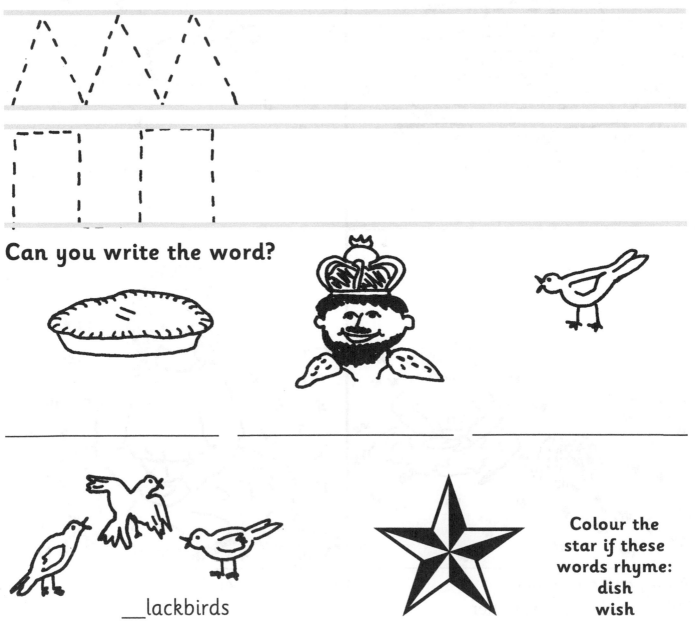

__lackbirds

Colour the
star if these
words rhyme:
dish
wish

# Sing a song of sixpence

**Colour the pictures.**
**Cut out the boxes with the words in.**
**Stick each box of words into the space under the picture it belongs to.**

| | |
|---|---|
| When the pie was open<br>The birds began to sing; | Wasn't that a dainty dish<br>To put before a king. |
| Sing a song of sixpence<br>A pocket full of rye; | Four and twenty blackbirds<br>Baked in a pie. |

# Ride a cock horse

Ride a cock horse
To Banbury Cross,
To see a fine lady upon a white horse;
With rings on her fingers
And bells on her toes
So she shall have music wherever she goes.

## Continue the pattern.

_____  _____  _____  _____

## Follow the lines to see who gets to Banbury Cross.

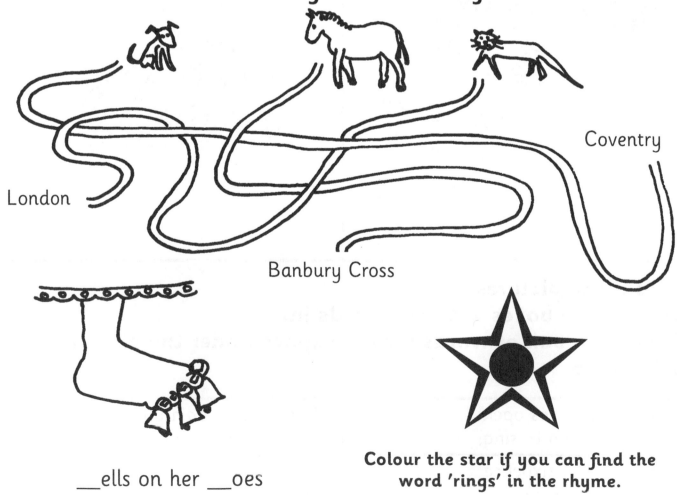

London

Coventry

Banbury Cross

__ells on her __oes

**Colour the star if you can find the word 'rings' in the rhyme.**

# Ride a cock horse

**Colour the pictures.**
**Cut them out and stick them in the right order.**

To see a fine lady upon a white horse;

Ride a cock horse
To Banbury Cross,

With rings on her fingers
And bells on her toes

So she shall have music wherever
she goes.

# Hickory, dickory dock

Hickory, dickory dock!
The mouse ran up the clock!
The clock struck one,
The mouse ran down,
Hickory, dickory dock!

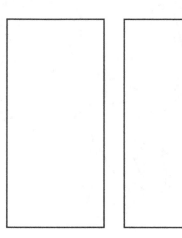

## Continue the pattern.

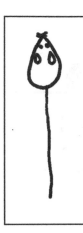 

## Can you write the word?

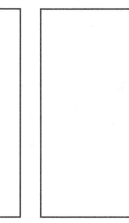

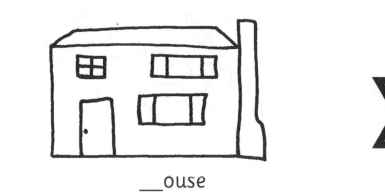

__ouse

Colour the
star if these
words rhyme:
mouse
house

# Hickory, dickory dock

**Colour the pictures.**
**Cut out the boxes with the words in.**
**Stick each box of words into the space under the picture it belongs to.**

| | |
|---|---|
| Hickory, dickory dock! | The clock struck one, |
| Hickory, dickory dock!<br>The mouse ran up the clock! | The mouse ran down, |

# Polly put the kettle on

Polly put the kettle on,
Polly put the kettle on,
Polly put the kettle on,
We'll all have tea.

Sukey take it off again,
Sukey take it off again,
Sukey take it off again,
They've all gone away.

**Circle the picture that is the same.**

**Trace the words.**

Polly put the kettle
on. Let's have tea.

__ettle

Colour the
star if you can
write a word
that rhymes
with 'tea'.

# Polly put the kettle on

**Colour the pictures.**
**Cut them out and stick them in the right order.**

Sukey take it off again,
They've all gone away.

Polly put the kettle on,
We'll all have tea.

Polly put the kettle on,
Polly put the kettle on,

Sukey take it off again,
Sukey take it off again,

# The grand old Duke of York

The grand old Duke of York,
He had ten thousand men;
He marched them up to the top of the hill
And he marched them down again.
And when they were up, they were up;
And when they were down, they were down;
And when they were only halfway up
They were neither up, nor down!

---

**Trace the words.**

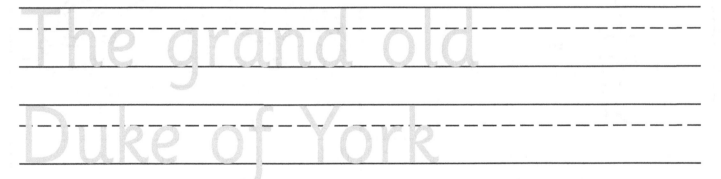

The grand old
Duke of York

**Draw the soldiers marching up.**

**Draw the soldiers marching down.**

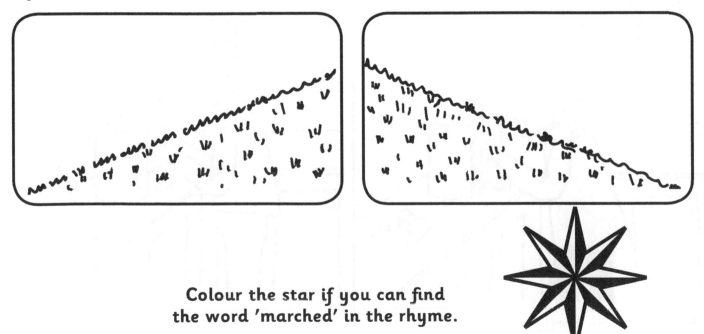

**Colour the star if you can find
the word 'marched' in the rhyme.**

---

# The grand old Duke of York

Colour the pictures.
Cut them out and stick them in the right order.

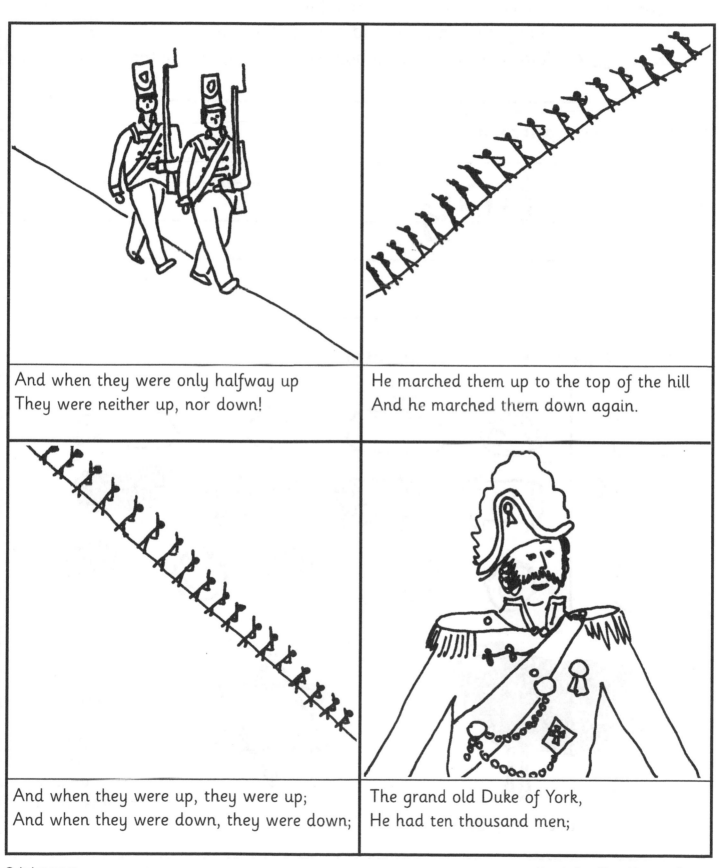

And when they were only halfway up
They were neither up, nor down!

He marched them up to the top of the hill
And he marched them down again.

And when they were up, they were up;
And when they were down, they were down;

The grand old Duke of York,
He had ten thousand men;

# Baa, baa, black sheep

Baa, baa, black sheep
Have you any wool?
Yes sir, yes sir, three bags full.
One for the master and one for the dame;
And one for the little boy who lives down the lane.

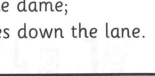

**Continue the pattern.**

## little boy little boy

**Circle the picture that is the same.**

__lack __ __eep

Colour the star if you can find a word in the rhyme that means 'lady'.

# Baa, baa, black sheep

**Colour the pictures.**
**Cut them out and stick them in the right order.**

Baa, baa, black sheep
Have you any wool?

And one for the little boy who lives down the lane.

One for the master and one for the dame;

Yes sir, yes sir, three bags full.

# Twinkle, twinkle, little star

Twinkle, twinkle, little star
How I wonder what you are;
Up above the world so high,
Like a diamond in the sky.

When the blazing sun is gone
When he nothing shines upon,
Then you show your little light,
Twinkle, twinkle, in the night.

## Circle the word that is the same.

| star | steal | save | she | star |
|------|-------|------|-----|------|
| light | night | light | late | little |
| sun | some | fun | sun | shoe |

## Continue the pattern.

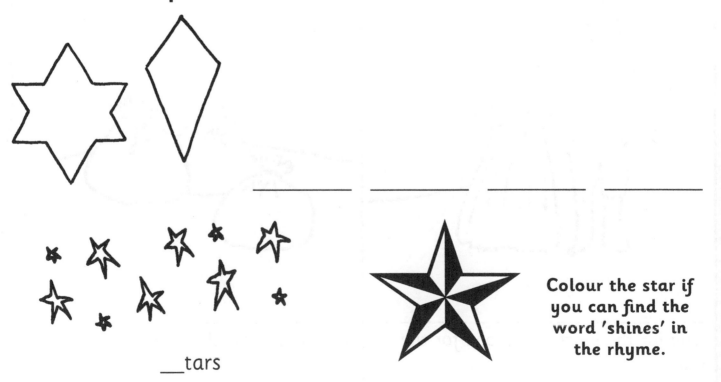

__tars

Colour the star if
you can find the
word 'shines' in
the rhyme.

# Twinkle, twinkle, little star

**Colour the pictures.**
**Cut them out and stick them in the right order.**

Twinkle, twinkle, little star
How I wonder what you are;

Then you show your little light,
Twinkle, twinkle, in the night.

Up above the world so high,
Like a diamond in the sky.

When the blazing sun is gone
When he nothing shines upon,

# Here we go round the Mulberry bush

Here we go round the Mulberry bush,
The Mulberry bush, the Mulberry bush;
Here we go round the Mulberry bush
On a cold and frosty morning.

This is the way we clap our hands
Clap our hands, clap our hands;
This is the way we clap our hands
On a cold and frosty morning.

**Trace and draw.**

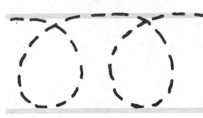

**Circle the word that is the same.**

| bush | brush | dust | bush | push |
|------|-------|------|------|------|
| clap | clip | clap | pick | lap |
| round | pound | down | road | round |

**Colour the star if these words rhyme:**
way
day
stay

# Here we go round the Mulberry bush

**Colour the pictures.**
**Cut them out and stick them in the right order.**

Here we go round the Mulberry bush,
The Mulberry bush, the Mulberry bush;

This is the way we clap our hands
Clap our hands, clap our hands;

Here we go round the Mulberry bush
On a cold and frosty morning.

This is the way we clap our hands
On a cold and frosty morning.

# Pop goes the weasel!

Half a pound of tuppenny rice,
Half a pound of treacle,
Mix it up and make it nice,
Pop goes the weasel!
Up and down the City Road
In and out of the Eagle –
That's the way the money goes –
Pop goes the weasel!

**Continue the pattern.**

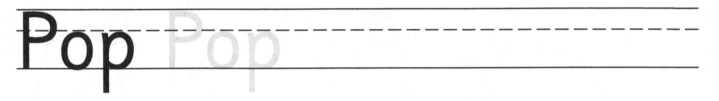

Pop Pop

**Circle the word that <u>rhymes</u>.**

| pop | got | shop | pod | dog |
|---|---|---|---|---|
| rice | mice | rich | mouse | mine |
| goes | gone | song | toes | gosh |

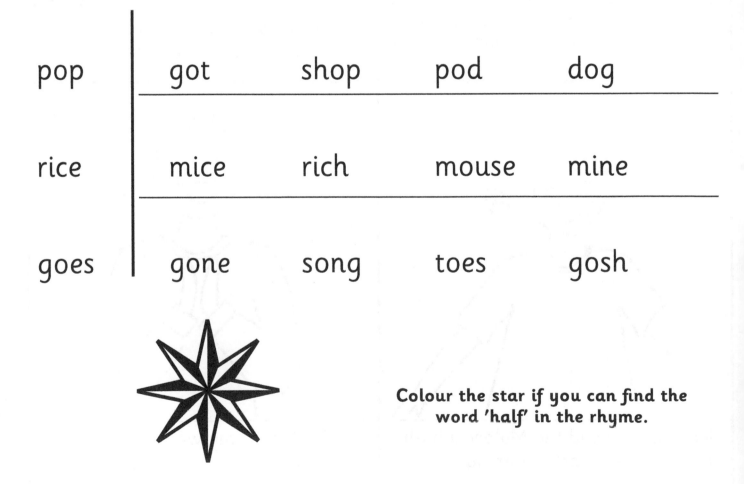

Colour the star if you can find the
word 'half' in the rhyme.

# Pop goes the weasel!

Colour the pictures.
Cut out the boxes with the words in.
Stick each box of words into the space under the picture it belongs to.

| | |
|---|---|
| Up and down the City Road<br>In and out of the Eagle – | Half a pound of tuppenny rice,<br>Half a pound of treacle, |
| Mix it up and make it nice,<br>Pop goes the weasel! | That's the way the money goes –<br>Pop goes the weasel! |

# Mary, Mary, quite contrary

"Mary, Mary, quite contrary,
How does your garden grow?"
"With silver bells and cockle shells,
And pretty maids all in a row."

## Can you write the word?

_____   _____   _____

## Circle the picture that is the same.

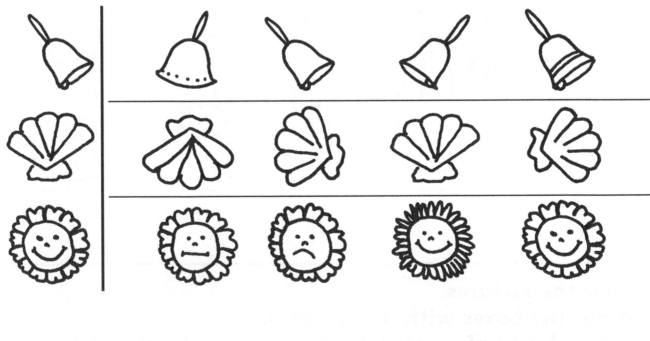

Colour the star if you can find the
word 'pretty' in the rhyme.

# Mary, Mary, quite contrary

**Colour the pictures.**
**Cut out the boxes with the words in.**
**Stick each box of words into the space under the picture it belongs to.**

| "Mary, Mary, quite contrary, | "With silver bells and cockle shells, |
|---|---|
| How does your garden grow?" | And pretty maids all in a row." |

# Little Jack Horner

Little Jack Horner
Sat in a corner
Eating his Christmas pie;
He stuck in his thumb
And pulled out a plum
And said, "What a good boy am I!"

**Join the dots.**

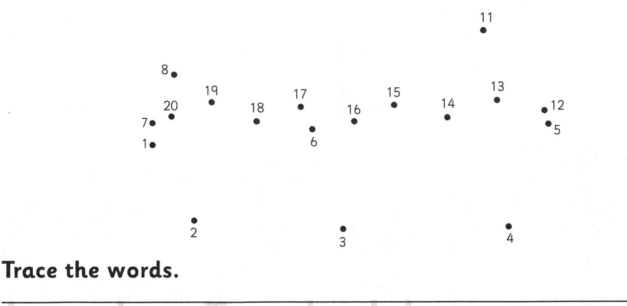

**Trace the words.**

Little Jack Horner

Colour the
star if you
can write a
word that
rhymes with
'sat'.

a __ __um on a __ __umb

# Little Jack Horner

**Colour the pictures.**
**Cut out the boxes with the words in.**
**Stick each box of words into the space under the picture it belongs to.**

| | |
|---|---|
| Little Jack Horner<br>Sat in a corner | And said, "What a good boy am I!" |
| He stuck in his thumb<br>And pulled out a plum | Eating his Christmas pie; |

# Old King Cole

Old King Cole
Was a merry old soul,
And a merry old soul was he;
He called for this pipe,
And he called for his drum,
And he called for his fiddlers three.

**Circle the word that <u>rhymes</u>.**

| Cole | coat | cool | hole | pail |
|------|------|------|------|------|
| drum | gum | drag | dear | moth |
| three | there | steep | with | tea |

**Finish the picture to make
Old King Cole look merry.**

**Colour the star if you can
find a word in the rhyme
that means 'happy'.**

# Old King Cole

**Colour the pictures.**
**Cut out the boxes with the words in.**
**Stick each box of words into the space under the picture it belongs to.**

| | |
|---|---|
| Old King Cole<br>Was a merry old soul, | And he called for his fiddlers three. |
| He called for this pipe,<br>And he called for his drum, | And a merry old soul was he; |

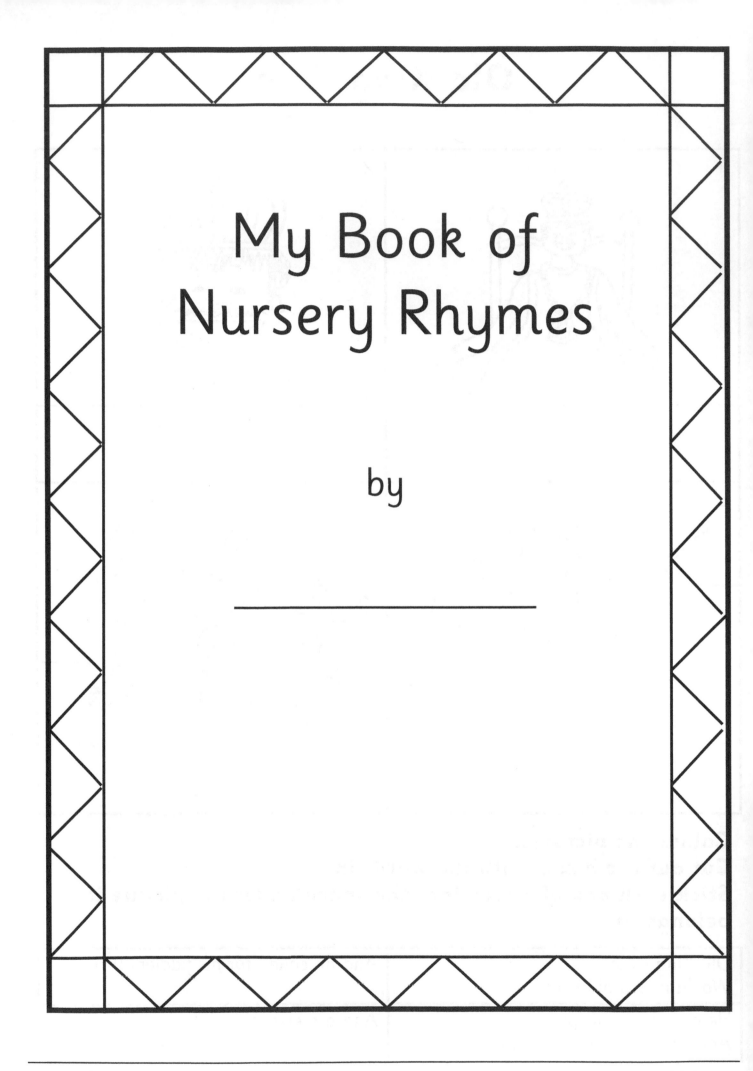

# My Book of Nursery Rhymes

by

_____

Lightning Source UK Ltd.
Milton Keynes UK
UKOW06f1706180913

217437UK00002B/57/P